THE GREAT BIBLE DISCOVERY

THE PROMISE

THE BIBLE IS A BEST-SELLER. IT IS ALSO ONE OF THE MASTER-WORKS OF WORLD LITERATURE - SO IMPORTANT THAT UNIVERSITIES TODAY TEACH 'NON-RELIGIOUS' BIBLE COURSES TO HELP STUDENTS WHO CHOOSE TO STUDY WESTERN LITERATURE.

THE BIBLE POSSESSES AN AMAZING POWER TO FASCINATE YOUNG AND OLD ALIKE.

ONE REASON FOR THIS UNIVERSAL APPEAL IS THAT IT DEALS WITH BASIC HUMAN LONGINGS, EMOTIONS, RELATIONSHIPS. 'ALL THE WORLD IS HERE.' ANOTHER REASON IS THAT SO MUCH OF THE BIBLE CONSISTS OF STORIES. THEY ARE FULL OF MEANING BUT EASY TO REMEMBER.

HERE ARE THOSE STORIES, PRESENTED SIMPLY AND WITH A MINIMUM OF EXPLANATION. WE HAVE LEFT THE TEXT TO SPEAK FOR ITSELF. GIFTED ARTISTS USE THE ACTION-STRIP TECHNIQUE TO BRING THE BIBLE'S DEEP MESSAGE TO READERS OF ALL AGES. THEIR DRAWINGS ARE BASED ON INFORMATION FROM ARCHAEOLOGICAL DISCOVERIES COVERING FIFTEEN CENTURIES.

AN ANCIENT BOOK - PRESENTED FOR THE PEOPLE OF THE SECOND MILLENNIUM. A RELIGIOUS BOOK - PRESENTED FREE FROM THE INTERPRETATION OF ANY PARTICULAR CHURCH. A UNIVERSAL BOOK - PRESENTED IN A FORM THAT ALL MAY ENJOY.

OM publishing
CARLISLE, UK

2

THE PROMISE

When Abraham left Ur, God promised that his descendants would be a great nation. After he had reached Canaan, a homeless wanderer, God made another promise: one day the land would belong to Abraham's children.

The story of Abraham, his son Isaac and his son Jacob, is a story of promises. How amazing that God should humble himself by making promises to humankind and bind himself by a covenant! It's not even as if the men and women concerned were wonderfully virtuous. The slave Hagar was first used to provide Abraham with the heir Sarah failed to produce and then thrown out of the 'family'. Jacob deceived his own father in order to secure the first-born's right to the blessings of the promise.

But Esau, who suffered from Jacob's sharp practice, showed in other ways that he did not value God's promise. Jacob, by contrast (and his mother Rebekah), took God and the promise seriously throughout his life. So did Abraham, who was even willing to sacrifice the son on whom he depended if God were to keep the promise of descendants. On this occasion his faith rose to the challenge, as it had when he had given his nephew Lot the right to the best land. (This was before the devastation of the area around what we now call the 'Dead' Sea.)

The way in which the stories are told is remarkably free from moral judgements. The Bible often records violent and immoral behaviour with little comment, if any. In the same way, it is often content merely to describe brave and faithful conduct. Readers are often left to draw their own conclusions - or ask their own questions. Sometimes we can see wrongdoing reaping its own harvest, as when Jacob, the deceiver, was cheated by his Uncle Laban. But by no means always.

The illustrations in this series are based on accurate research into the way buildings and clothes changed according to time and place, from Egypt and Mesopotamia and finally into the worlds of Greece and Rome. These changes may also remind us that the men and women in these stories inhabited a different world from ours. God was the same, of course. But they thought of him in their way, not ours.

GENESIS 12 - 36

First published as *Découvrir la Bible* 1983

First edition © Librairie Larousse 1983
English translation © Daan Retief Publishers 1990
24-volume series adaptation by Mike Jacklin © Knowledge Unlimited 1994
This edition © OM Publishing 1995

01 00 99 98 97 96 95   7 6 5 4 3 2 1

OM Publishing is an imprint of Send the Light Ltd.,
P.O. Box 300, Carlisle, Cumbria CA3 0QS, U.K.

Series editor: D. Roy Briggs
English translation: Bethan Uden
Introductions: Peter Cousins

British Library Cataloguing in Publication Data
A catalogue record for this book is available from the British Library
ISBN 1-85078-206-7

Printed in Singapore by Tien Wah Press (Pte) Ltd.

ABRAHAM
part 2

WHILE HE WAS AT THE OAKS OF MAMRE, ABRAHAM WAS VISITED BY THREE MESSENGERS. THEY WERE VERY ANGRY WITH SODOM. WHEN ABRAHAM DEFENDED THE TOWN, THEY MADE THIS AGREEMENT WITH HIM: IF THEY FOUND TEN GOOD PEOPLE IN SODOM, THEY WOULD NOT DESTROY IT. TWO OF THEM TRAVELLED TO SODOM.

OUTSIDE THE WALLS OF SODOM LOT WAS ENJOYING THE PEACE OF THE EVENING...

...WHEN THE TWO MESSENGERS ARRIVED...

SIRS, DO ME THE HONOUR OF SPENDING THE NIGHT IN MY HOUSE.

LET'S GO THIS WAY. IT'S MORE SECLUDED.

STORY: Etienne DAHLER.   DRAWING: Victor de la FUENTE

NO PROBLEM! WE'RE SAFE HERE.

TELL US, LOT, ARE THERE TEN GOOD PEOPLE IN THIS CITY?

PERHAPS, BUT LIKE ME, THEY KEEP TO THEMSELVES.

LOT SPOKE AT LENGTH ABOUT THE SIN OF SODOM.

LOT, THE WHOLE CITY'S AT OUR DOOR. THEY'LL KILL US... BECAUSE OF THEM...

WE SAW THEM, LOT!

BRING OUT YOUR VISITORS!

I KNOW HOW TO HONOUR THEM!

BRING THEM HERE. LET'S HAVE SOME FUN!

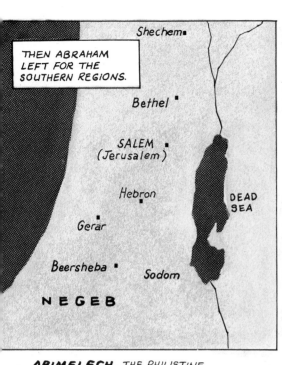

THEN ABRAHAM LEFT FOR THE SOUTHERN REGIONS.

Shechem•

Bethel •

SALEM (Jerusalem) •

Hebron •

DEAD SEA

Gerar •

Beersheba •   Sodom

NEGEB

ARRIVING AMONGST THE PHILISTINES, ABRAHAM AGAIN LET IT BE KNOWN THAT SARAH WAS HIS SISTER. IN ALL GOOD FAITH...

... **ABIMELECH,** THE PHILISTINE KING, CARRIED HER OFF.

THE FOLLOWING NIGHT IN A DREAM...

ABIMELECH, YOU'LL DIE, BECAUSE THIS WOMAN HAS A HUSBAND.

I DIDN'T KNOW. I ACTED WITH A PURE HEART.

GIVE HER BACK TO ABRAHAM.

WHY DID YOU MAKE ME COMMIT SO GREAT A WRONG?
COME HERE...

THE NEXT DAY...

WHAT WERE YOU THINKING OF TO BEHAVE LIKE THIS?

I SAID TO MYSELF: THESE PEOPLE DON'T BELIEVE IN GOD. TO GET A WOMAN, A MAN WOULD EVEN KILL HER HUSBAND.

IT'S ALL MY FAULT! SARAH IS MY WIFE AS WELL AS BEING MY HALF-SISTER.

TAKE SARAH BACK, AND ACCEPT THESE PRESENTS AS WELL...
MY COUNTRY'S YOURS; STAY WHEREVER YOU LIKE.

MAY GOD BLESS YOU AND ALL YOUR HOUSEHOLD.

* ISAAC

9

THE YEARS PASSED...

WHAT A GRAND FEAST IN HONOUR OF YOUR SON!

YES. BUT... SARAH, WHERE'S ISAAC? HAVE HIM BROUGHT HERE.

HE MUST BE PLAYING WITH THE OTHER CHILDREN. I'LL CALL HIM.

ISAAC!

ISHMAEL'S ALWAYS MISTREATING ISAAC... SO SEND AWAY THIS SLAVE-WOMAN AND HER SON...

...AND MY SON.

11

HAGAR WALKED FOR MANY HOURS. SHE GOT LOST. THE SUN BLINDED HER. HER WATERSKIN WAS EMPTY.

ISHMAEL, I'M SURE WE'LL FIND A WATER-HOLE.

I DON'T WANT TO SEE MY CHILD DIE!

I... I'M THIRSTY... FATHER...!

ISHMAEL'S CRY WAS HEARD...

GE

YOU'LL FIND A SPRING A FEW KILOMETRES TO THE WEST.

THEY WENT TO LIVE IN THE ARABIAN DESERT...

ISHMAEL HAD TWELVE SONS:

NEBAIOTH, KEDAR, ADBEEL, MIBSAM, MISHMA, DUMAH, MASSA, HADAD, TEMAN, JETUR, NAPHISH, KEDEMAH.

NOW, AS A POTTER TESTS HIS POTS, KEEPING THE GOOD AND BREAKING THE FAULTY ONES, GOD ONCE MORE TESTED ABRAHAM.

TAKE YOUR SON, ISAAC, THE ONE YOU LOVE; GO TO THE LAND OF MORIAH, AND OFFER HIM AS A SACRIFICE ON THE MOUNTAIN I WILL SHOW YOU.

WHY DOES GOD ASK SUCH A THING OF ME...

...I WHO HAVE ALWAYS CONDEMNED THE IDOLATORS FOR THEIR HUMAN SACRIFICES...

After walking for three days, Abraham scanned the horizon...

Then Abraham saw a ram and offered it on the fire instead of his son.

SARAH'S **JUST DIED.** GO QUICKLY AND TELL THE MASTER IN BEERSHEBA.

AT HEBRON, A LITTLE LATER...

I WANT A PLACE TO BURY **SARAH.**

TO THE LEADING MEN OF HEBRON...

ABRAHAM, YOU'RE A LEADER FROM GOD AMONGST US. CHOOSE ONE OF OUR TOMBS.

THE PATRIARCH ASKED FOR THE CAVE OF MACHPELAH. HE BOUGHT IT: **THE FIRST PIECE OF THE PROMISED LAND.**

BY THIS ACT I GIVE ALL MY BELONGINGS TO ISAAC. BUT REMEMBER, HE MUST NEVER LEAVE *THE PROMISED LAND.*

MY MASTER, I SWEAR IT TO YOU!

COME BACK QUICKLY! ...OTHERWISE I'LL NEVER KNOW HER...

HEBRON — HARAN: ABOUT 30 DAYS ON FOOT.

WE'RE APPROACHING HARAN. LET'S LOOK FOR A WATER-HOLE THAT'S THE PLACE TO HEAR THE LATEST NEWS.

NEAR THE WELL, ELIEZER ASKS THE LORD FOR A SIGN.

WILL I FIND HER HERE?... *AND HOW WILL I RECOGNIZE HER?*

LORD, GOD OF ABRAHAM... THE YOUNG GIRL TO WHOM I SAY *'LOWER YOUR JAR TO LET ME DRINK...'*

AND WHO REPLIES *'DRINK, AND I'LL WATER YOUR CAMELS TOO...'*

BLESSED BE THE ETERNAL GOD WHO BROUGHT ME RIGHT TO MY MASTER'S FAMILY...!

Rebecca ran home to tell them about her meeting...

I'M LABAN, BROTHER OF REBECCA WHO GAVE YOU A DRINK. DON'T PITCH YOUR TENT! COME TO OUR HOME...

SPEAK!

In his turn, Eliezer told his story. Bethuel, the young girl's father, listened to him.

ALL THIS COMES FROM GOD. LET REBECCA BE THE WIFE OF YOUR MASTER'S SON.

DO YOU AGREE TO GO WITH THIS MAN, REBECCA?

YES FATHER. I COULD LEAVE TOMORROW.

HERE ARE PRESENTS FROM MY MASTER.

GOOD! NOW LET'S EAT!

SARAH'S DEATH HAD
SADDENED ISAAC.
BUT THAT EVENING...

BACK ALREADY?

STOP!

A MAN IN THE DISTANCE. HE'S COMING THIS WAY. HE'S RUNNING. ISN'T HE THE SON OF YOUR MASTER?

YES! IT'S ISAAC!

THIS IS REBECCA, THE DAUGHTER OF BETHUEL.

MY LORD!

REBECCA, YOU'VE BEEN FOUND WORTHY TO GIVE ABRAHAM HEIRS.

REBECCA WILL BE THE MOTHER OF THOUSANDS...

NOW I CAN PEACEFULLY GO TO BE WITH SARAH. EVERYTHING'S YOURS, ISAAC... *AND ALSO THE PROMISE GOD GAVE ME.*

THE WEDDING OF ISAAC AND REBECCA CAUSED GREAT JOY IN THE HOUSE OF ABRAHAM.

TEACH YOUR CHILDREN THESE THINGS. MAKE SURE THEY FAITHFULLY SERVE THE MOST HIGH.

SO THE YEARS WENT BY.

ISAAC PRAYED SILENTLY. HE HAD NO CHILDREN.

THE CHILDREN GREW UP.
ESAU BECAME A SKILLED AND
CUNNING HUNTER.
JACOB WAS A QUIET MAN,
WHO SPENT HIS DAYS
AROUND THE TENTS.

MY GOD,
YOU'VE BLESSED ME
FAR BEYOND
MY HOPES.

THEN, AT A GREAT AGE, ABRAHAM DIED...

HIS SONS AND
GRANDSONS CARRIED
HIM TO THE CAVE OF
MACHPELAH, WHERE
SARAH WAS BURIED.

ISHMAEL,
LET'S NEVER FORGET
THAT HE WAS FATHER
TO BOTH OF US.

YES, **ISAAC,**
OUR DESCENDANTS
MUST ALWAYS
REMEMBER
THAT!

ISAAC and JACOB

STORY: Etienne DAHLER
DRAWING: Raymond POÏVET

THERE WAS A FAMINE
IN CANAAN,
LIKE THAT IN THE TIME
OF ABRAHAM.

FOLLOWING THE EXAMPLE
OF HIS FATHER, ISAAC
DECIDED TO BREAK CAMP
AND GO TO EGYPT.

DO NOT GO DOWN
INTO EGYPT.
STAY IN THIS LAND.
I WILL BE WITH YOU
AND I WILL KEEP THE
PROMISE MADE TO
YOUR FATHER
ABRAHAM.

ISAAC OBEYED...
HE STAYED IN CANAAN...

AFTER ENDLESS DAYS OF
UNBEARABLE DROUGHT,
THE RAIN CAME
TO GIVE HIS
PEOPLE
LIFE.

...AND FORTUNE
SMILED ON HIM.
HE HARVESTED
100 TIMES
MORE THAN
HE HAD SOWN.

... RICHER THAN ALL OF US PUT TOGETHER. HE TAKES OUR LAND AND THE WATER FROM OUR SPRINGS. ARE WE GOING TO LET HIM **HAVE THE WHOLE COUNTRY?**

THE PEOPLE OF THE COUNTRY ARE JEALOUS OF ISAAC'S SUCCESS.

... THE THIRD WELL WE'VE FILLED IN SINCE THIS MORNING...

HIS REACTION WILL BE TERRIBLE...

MASTER, WE'RE THE STRONGEST. ONE WORD FROM YOU AND THEY'RE IN OUR HANDS.

NO! LET'S WITHDRAW AND WAIT UNTIL THEIR ANGER'S DIED DOWN.

THE NEWS WAS TAKEN TO ISAAC...

ISAAC LEFT THERE, CAMPING IN THE VALLEY OF GERAR. THEN HE MOVED TO BEERSHEBA...

... AND SETTLED THERE. THEY SET ABOUT DIGGING A WELL. ONE DAY ISAAC SAW ABIMELECH, THE KING, COMING TOWARDS HIM. HE HAD LEFT GERAR, ACCOMPANIED BY PHICOL, THE COMMANDER OF HIS ARMY.

WHY COME TO ME, IF YOU HATE ME? YOU CHASED ME OUT OF YOUR COUNTRY...

IT'S PLAIN TO US THAT GOD'S WITH YOU, ISAAC. **WE'VE COME TO MAKE PEACE WITH YOU.**

AND THEY SWORE AN OATH. THE NEXT DAY, ABIMELCH HAD JUST GONE, WHEN...

...THE WELL... IT'S HERE, MASTER! WATER! * AT SHIBAH...!

*The name means 'oath'.

AFTER THAT ISAAC LIVED PEACEFULLY AT BEERSHEBA.

ESAU, HIS SON, MARRIED TWO HITTITE GIRLS, JUDITH AND BASEMATH.

MY SON, I'M GOING TO DIE SOON... GO HUNTING AND PREPARE ME A DISH OF VENISON. **I'LL GIVE YOU MY BLESSING AS THE FIRST-BORN.**

IN HIS OLD AGE ISAAC BECAME BLIND. ONE DAY HE CALLED ESAU...

YOU MUST ACT QUICKLY, JACOB! YOUR FATHER'S GOING TO BLESS ESAU; THEN THERE'LL BE NOTHING MORE WE CAN DO.

BUT REBECCA OVERHEARD.

GO AND GET ME TWO GOATS FROM THE HERD. I'LL MAKE ONE OF YOUR FATHER'S FAVOURITE DISHES.

JACOB OBEYED.

REBECCA TOOK A GOATSKIN...

IT WAS VERY LATE WHEN ESAU RETURNED.

HE'S TRICKED ME TWICE, FATHER! FIRST THE BIRTHRIGHT, AND NOW THE BLESSING!

ESAU CRIED BECAUSE HIS BROTHER JACOB HAD STOLEN HIS BLESSING.

JACOB, YOUR BROTHER WANTS VENGEANCE. HE WANTS TO KILL YOU. GO TO MY BROTHER LABAN. WAIT THERE UNTIL HIS ANGER COOLS DOWN.

ISAAC, JACOB MUST HAVE A WIFE. BUT NOT A HITTITE WIFE! I'M TIRED OF ESAU'S WIVES...

BUT MY PLACE IS HERE, WHATEVER THE DANGER.

TRUE. JACOB MY CHILD, DON'T TAKE A CANAANITE WIFE; GO TO HARAN AND CHOOSE ONE OF LABAN'S DAUGHTERS...

I AM THE LORD,
THE GOD OF ABRAHAM AND ISAAC.

I WILL GIVE THE GROUND ON WHICH YOU SLEEP TO YOU AND YOUR DESCENDANTS.

MY BLESSING WILL BE ON YOU, AND, THROUGH YOU, ON ALL THE FAMILIES OF THE EARTH.

I AM WITH YOU..
WHEREVER YOU GO
I WILL GUARD YOU.

THE LORD'S HERE, AND I DIDN'T KNOW IT.

WAKING UP...

JACOB RAISED THE STONE HE'D SLEPT ON AS AN ALTAR, AND POURED OIL ON IT. HE CALLED THE PLACE BETHEL*

LET THIS STONE BE THE FOUNDATION OF THE HOUSE OF GOD.

* House of God.

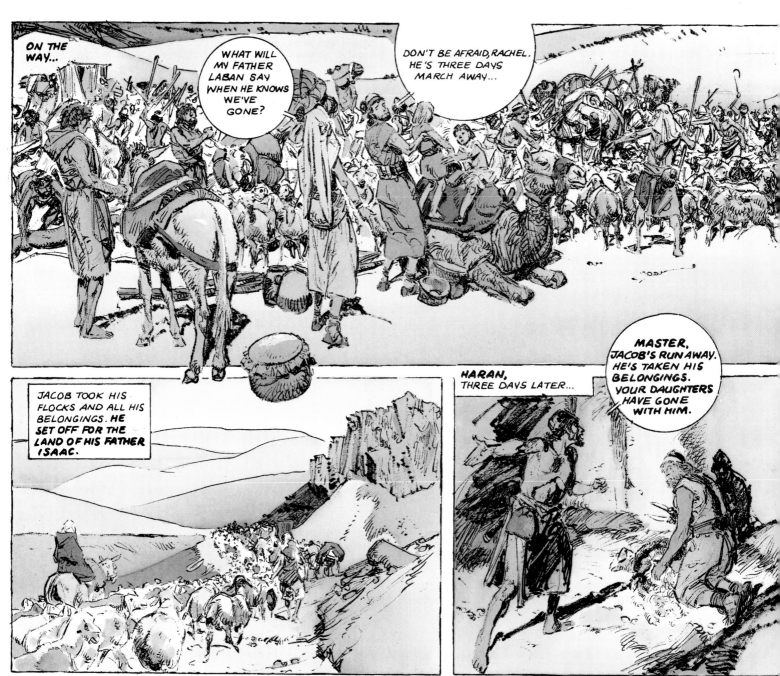

ON THE WAY...

WHAT WILL MY FATHER LABAN SAY WHEN HE KNOWS WE'VE GONE?

DON'T BE AFRAID, RACHEL. HE'S THREE DAYS MARCH AWAY...

JACOB TOOK HIS FLOCKS AND ALL HIS BELONGINGS. HE SET OFF FOR THE LAND OF HIS FATHER ISAAC.

HARAN, THREE DAYS LATER...

MASTER, JACOB'S RUN AWAY. HE'S TAKEN HIS BELONGINGS. YOUR DAUGHTERS HAVE GONE WITH HIM.

HE WON'T TRAVEL VERY FAST WITH THE ANIMALS...

LABAN IMMEDIATELY SET OFF TO THE SOUTH AFTER JACOB.

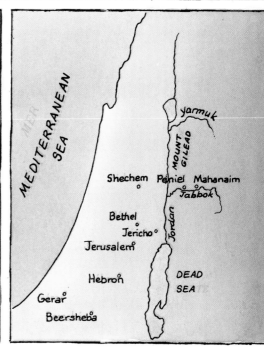

MEDITERRANEAN SEA

Yarmuk

MOUNT GILEAD

Shechem Peniel Mahanaim
Jabbok

Bethel
Jericho
Jerusalem

Hebron   DEAD SEA

Gerar

Beersheba

Jordan

LABAN FOUND NOTHING IN RACHEL'S TENT...

FORGIVE ME FOR NOT GETTING UP IN YOUR PRESENCE, FATHER; I'M NOT WELL.

...SHE'D HIDDEN THEM UNDERNEATH HER.

JACOB DIDN'T KNOW THAT RACHEL HAD STOLEN THEM BEFORE LEAVING...

WHY FOLLOW ME LIKE THIS? AFTER 20 YEARS OF WORK! HAVE YOU FOUND ANYTHING HERE THAT BELONGS TO YOU?

LABAN HAD TO GIVE UP. HE SUGGESTED AN AGREEMENT TO JACOB...

I TAKE THIS STONE YOU'VE RAISED AS A WITNESS. I SHAN'T BREAK MY WORD AND GO AGAINST YOU, NOR YOU AGAINST ME, JACOB.

I SWEAR IT BY THE GOD OF MY FATHER ISAAC.

LABAN LEFT MOUNT GILEAD AND RETURNED TO HARAN.

* Mahanaim means 'the two camps'.

ALONE AT THE FORD OF JABBOK...

... SOMEONE WRESTLED WITH HIM UNTIL DAYBREAK...

LET ME GO; IT'S GETTING LIGHT.

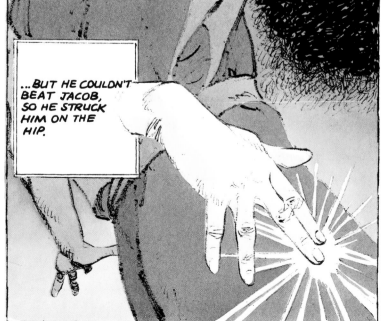

...BUT HE COULDN'T BEAT JACOB, SO HE STRUCK HIM ON THE HIP.

YOU SHAN'T GO WITHOUT BLESSING ME!

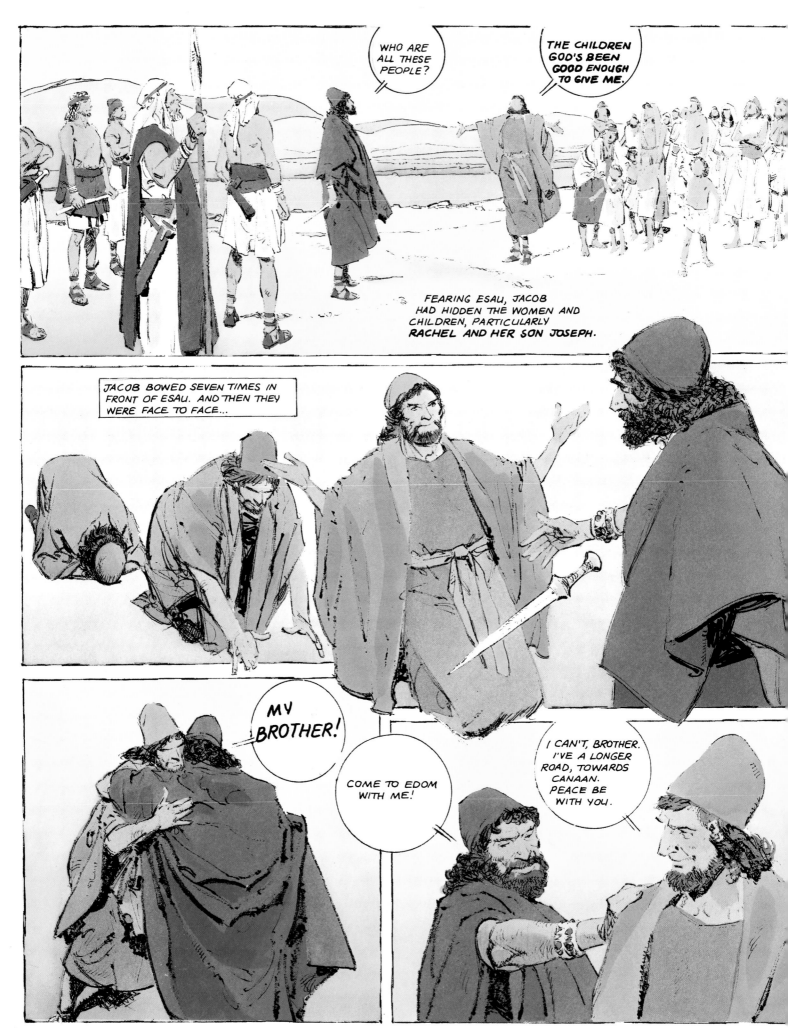

46

JACOB SETTLED AT SHECHEM FOR MANY YEARS.

LET'S GO TO BETHEL AND THANK THE LORD THAT WE LIVE IN PEACE.

BUT FIRST GET RID OF YOUR FOREIGN GODS. **WE MUST PURIFY OURSELVES!**

JACOB BURIED ALL THE IDOLS UNDER THE OAK-TREE NEAR SHECHEM. THEN HE SET OFF...

...FOR BETHEL. THERE GOD HAD APPEARED TO HIM IN A DREAM IN HIS YOUTH, AND GIVEN HIM A PROMISE...

I WILL GIVE YOU THE LAND I PROMISED TO ABRAHAM AND ISAAC, AND I WILL GIVE IT TO YOUR DESCENDANTS AFTER YOU.